lonely planet KIDS

THE
GAMES on the GO
ACTIVITY BOOK

T0027356

ACKNOWLEDGEMENTS

Author: Christina Webb
Illustrator: Andy Mansfield
Publishing Director: Piers Pickard
Publisher: Rebecca Hunt
Editorial Director: Joe Fullman
Art Director: Andy Mansfield
Print Production: Nigel Longuet

Published in April 2024 by
Lonely Planet Global Limited
CRN: 554153
ISBN: 978 1 83758 222 8
www.lonelyplanet.com/kids
© Lonely Planet 2024

10 9 8 7 6 5 4 3 2 1

Printed in China

MIX
Paper from
responsible sources
FSC™ C021741

Paper in this book is certified against the
Forest Stewardship Council™ standards.
FSC™ promotes environmentally responsible,
socially beneficial and economically viable
management of the world's forests.

THE
GAMES on the GO
ACTIVITY BOOK

This book is packed full of amazing travel-themed activities to tackle on long trips and rainy days. Solve mazes, answer riddles, take on sketching challenges, spot odd ones out, and much more. Each puzzle is designed to get you thinking and take your mind on its own fun-packed journey. Be sure to share the excitement by getting your friends and family to help out. If you get stuck, there's a page at the back for figuring things out. The answers start on page 146. No peeking!

STAY IN TOUCH

lonelyplanet.com/contact

Lonely Planet Office:

IRELAND
Digital Depot, Roe Lane
(off Thomas St.), Digital Hub,
Dublin 8, D08 TCV4, Ireland

ROAD TRIP* BINGO

Mark the pictures as you spot these items on your journey. You can play by yourself or with a friend. Complete a row, a column, or the whole board to win!

fir tree		tow truck
	stroller	
detour sign		dog on a leash
	traffic light	
flag flying		cat
	police car	
bicycle		delivery truck
	bird on the ground	

movie theater

helicopter

worker in a hard hat

church with a spire

scooter

gas station

traffic cone

motorbike

sheep

no entry sign

horse

horse in trailer

airplane

tractor

fire engine

mail van

sailboat

camper

butterfly

animal road sign

5

A WHOLE NEW
BALL GAME

How many balls can you find in this scene? Use your pencil to circle them, then write your answer in the space below.

Answer:

MIRROR
MIRROR

Complete these vacation pictures.
The right-hand side of each image
should be the same as the left.
Use the grid as a guide.

TOP (LAND) MARKS

Can you match the name of each of the landmarks in the list on the right with the images on these pages? Write your answers in the spaces.

1 _____

2 _____

3 _____

4 _____

5 _____

6 _____

7 _____

8 _____

- ACROPOLIS, GREECE
- ANGKOR WAT, CAMBODIA
- BURJ KHALIFA, UAE
- CHICHÉN ITZA, MEXICO
- CHRIST THE REDEEMER STATUE, BRAZIL
- COLOSSEUM, ITALY
- EIFFEL TOWER, FRANCE
- GREAT WALL OF CHINA
- MOUNT RUSHMORE, USA
- PYRAMIDS OF GIZA, EGYPT
- SAGRADA FAMILIA, SPAIN
- STATUE OF LIBERTY, USA
- SYDNEY OPERA HOUSE, AUSTRALIA
- TABLE MOUNTAIN, SOUTH AFRICA
- TAJ MAHAL, INDIA
- TOWER BRIDGE, UK

9 _____

10 _____

11 _____

12 _____

13 _____

14 _____

15 _____

16 _____

See solution on p.146

BLANK CHECK

Can you fill in the blank space in each of these travel facts with the correct word from the three options available?

1 In London, getting around is easy if you jump on a bright

_____
(blue/red/green)
double-decker bus.

2 New York is famous for its

_____
(red/purple/yellow)
taxis.

3 In Venice, a popular way to travel on the canals is by

_____
(gondola/bathtub/yacht)

4 The *Titanic* was the world's largest

_____
(submarine/ship/helicopter)
when it launched in 1912.

5 The first airplane flight was made in 1903 by the

_____
(Wright/Wrong/Maybe)
brothers.

6 Huskies pull people and goods on

_____
(hovercrafts/bicycles/sleds)
in snowy regions.

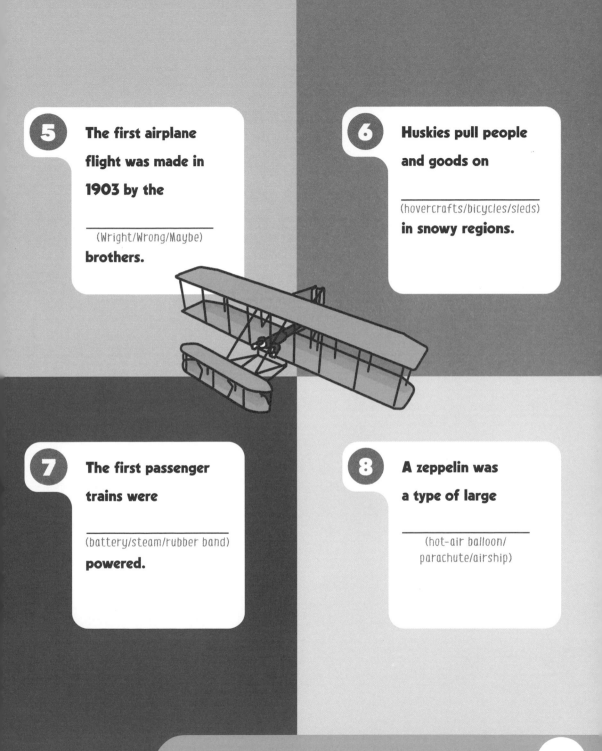

7 The first passenger trains were

_____
(battery/steam/rubber band)
powered.

8 A zeppelin was a type of large

_____
(hot-air balloon/
parachute/airship)

See solution on p.146

IT'S NO PICNIC

omplete the puzzle so that each row, column, and box of four small squares contains just one of each picnic item.

See solution on p.146

CONTINENT
CONTENT

Can you match each of the continents with its fact?
Write the correct number in each circle.

1 You'll find the Amazon rainforest here.

2 This continent is home to the Sahara, the largest hot desert in the world.

3 More than half the world's people live on this massive continent.

4 This continent includes the northern region of Scandinavia.

○ ASIA

○ SOUTH AMERICA

○ AFRICA

○ EUROPE

See solution on p.146

SQUARED UP*

How many squares can you
see in this picture? Write
your answer in the box below.

Answer:

See solution on p.146

TOWER ABOVE

Buildings are getting taller and taller, with new record-breaking skyscrapers being constructed every year. Draw your own skyscrapers to tower over this skyline.

JUST DESERTS

Can you tell which of these statements about deserts are true? Check the correct column!

		TRUE	FALSE
1	Deserts cover about a fifth of Earth's land surface.	○	○
2	All deserts are covered in sand.	○	○
3	The Sahara Desert is roughly the same size as the United States.	○	○
4	It never snows in deserts.	○	○
5	There are areas of desert where no rainfall has ever been recorded.	○	○

		TRUE	FALSE

6 The temperature can drop below freezing in hot deserts at night.

7 Flooding never occurs in deserts.

8 Deserts are too hot for people to live in.

9 Deserts are found on every continent.

10 Cacti grow in every desert.

OUT OF THE AIR

A re you ready to take to the skies with this air travel word search? Words can be found horizontally, vertically, diagonally, forward, or backward!

```
V L A N I M R E T W
V K X P I U E S Q T
U F C L E C B E U R
O L P A I Z S V H O
V I E N P A L Q J P
H G R E C K S I R S
B H N T X R C X A S
S T I C K E T A Y A
Q U Y X I V W T B P
S S F J B T O X X D
```

Suitcase	Plane	Ticket	Passport
Terminal	Taxi	Backpack	Flight

 See solution on p.146

TAKE A VIEW

Draw what you can see outside your window—whether you're looking at clouds from a plane, mountains from a train, or houses from your car. Be quick—sketch the scene before it passes you by!

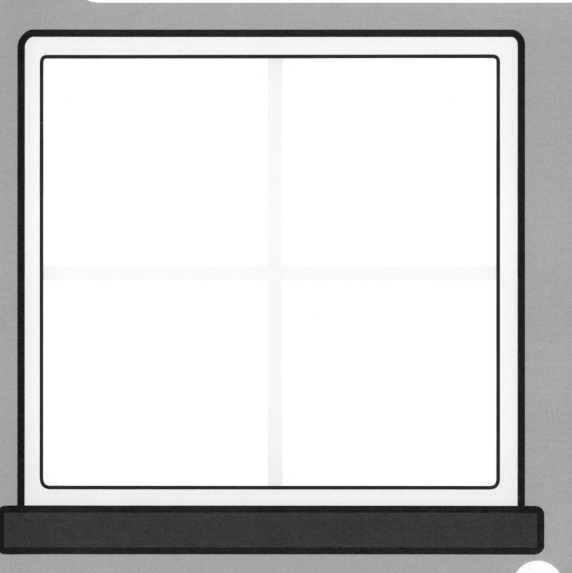

NUMBERS UP*

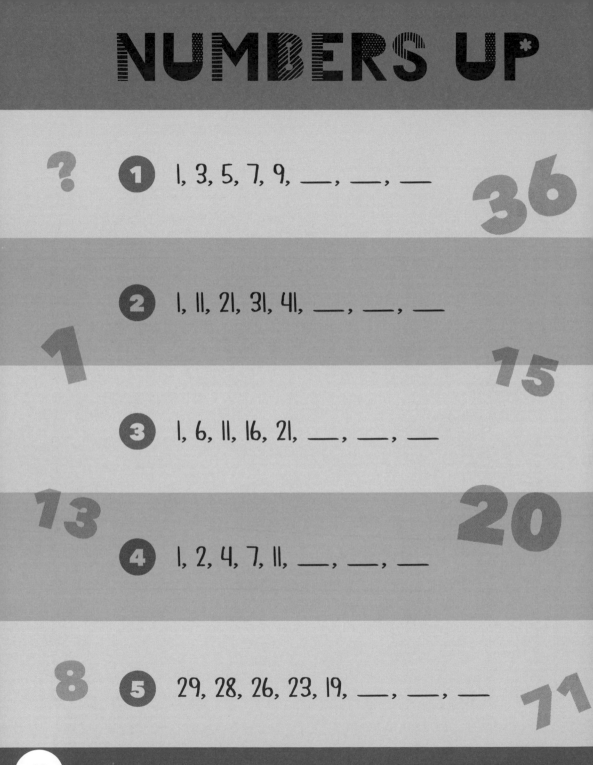

1 1, 3, 5, 7, 9, ___, ___, ___

2 1, 11, 21, 31, 41, ___, ___, ___

3 1, 6, 11, 16, 21, ___, ___, ___

4 1, 2, 4, 7, 11, ___, ___, ___

5 29, 28, 26, 23, 19, ___, ___, ___

**Figure out what comes
next in these sequences!**

6 1, 1, 2, 3, 5, 8, ___, ___, ___   96

?

7 3, 6, 12, 24, 48, ___, ___, ___

243

8 57, 50, 43, 36, 29, ___, ___, ___

?

9 1, 3, 9, 27, 81, ___, ___, ___

22

10 512, 256, 128, 64, 32, ___, ___, ___   1

See solution on p.146

FEATURE CREATURE

Strange monsters lurk deep in the jungle. Draw a crazy creature coming toward you through the trees in the space below.

PACK IT IN

All of these items are going to be packed into this suitcase. Try to memorize them all, then turn the page to see how many you can recall.

AWAY FROM THE PACK

The items have now been packed, but one didn't fit and has been left behind. Can you figure out which one?

See solution on p.147

FACE VALUE

Draw a portrait of someone who did a kind thing for you today! List their name or title in the rectangle below.

Can you spot 10 differences between these two camping scenes? Circle each difference.

LOST LUGGAGE

Can you help this traveler find his bag at the airport? He knows that...

- It doesn't have a round handle.

- It does have wheels.

- It doesn't have a triangular sticker.

- It does have an even number of zippers.

See solution on p.147

FROM THE SOURCE

Can you figure out which river ends up at which port?

STUCK IN TRAFFIC

Can you figure out which of these tiles doesn't appear in this street scene?

1

2

3

4

See solution on p.147

SHIP*SHAPE

Can you figure out which silhouette is an exact match of this ship?

JEWEL SCHOOL

Each set of scales holds jewels of equal weights on each side. What jewels should be placed on the right-hand side of scale 4 to make it balance?

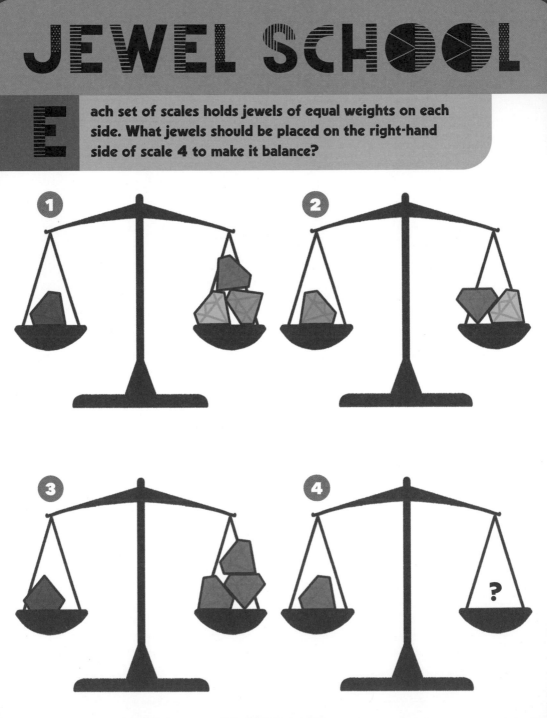

See solution on p.147

CHECK IN

Try to take in as much of this image as you can. Then turn the page to see how much you can remember.

CHECK OUT

See what you can recall about the previous scene. Circle your answers.

1 What time did the clock say?

A) 1 o'clock B) 3 o'clock C) 6 o'clock

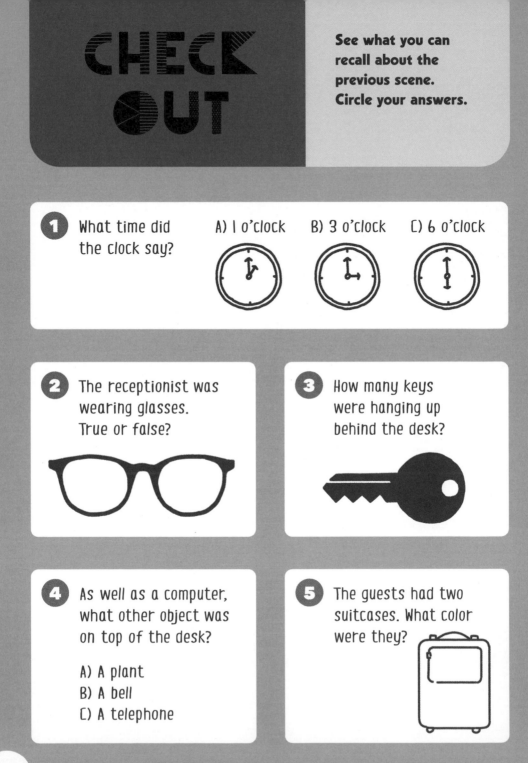

2 The receptionist was wearing glasses. True or false?

3 How many keys were hanging up behind the desk?

4 As well as a computer, what other object was on top of the desk?

A) A plant
B) A bell
C) A telephone

5 The guests had two suitcases. What color were they?

See solution on p.147

WiNGiNG IT

Can you find the butterfly that doesn't have identical wings? Look closely!

FIX YOUR WAGON

Draw the vehicle you think these wheels belong to. Is it a car, a motorbike, a bus, a train, a plane, a safari jeep, or something else entirely?

THAT'S CAPITAL

Can you find these eight capital cities in the word search? Words can be found horizontally, vertically, diagonally, forward, or backward!

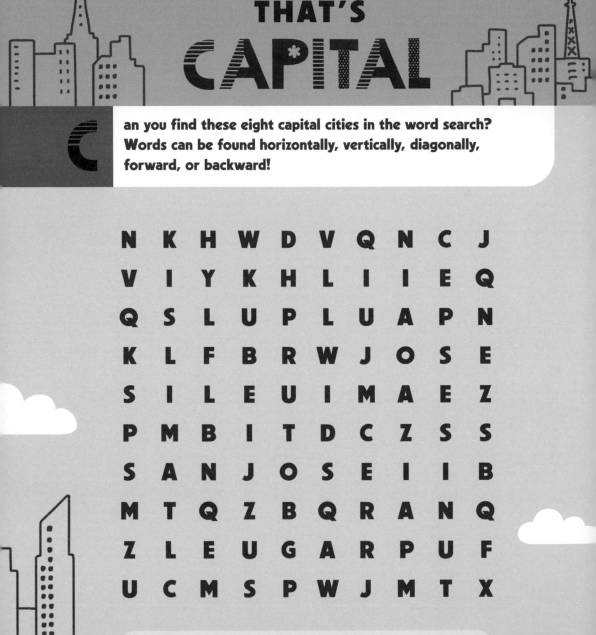

```
N K H W D V Q N C J
V I Y K H L I I E Q
Q S L U P L U A P N
K L F B R W J O S E
S I L E U I M A E Z
P M B I T D C Z S S
S A N J O S E I I B
M T Q Z B Q R A N Q
Z L E U G A R P U F
U C M S P W J M T X
```

Paris	Prague	Seoul	Lima
San Jose	Berlin	Dublin	Tunis

See solution on p.148

PLANE AND SIMPLE

Draw a path through the maze of roads, avoiding all vehicles, to help this family get to their plane.

FINISH

START ▶

See solution on p.148

III FLAG UP* III

Draw lines to connect each of these flags with its correct country.

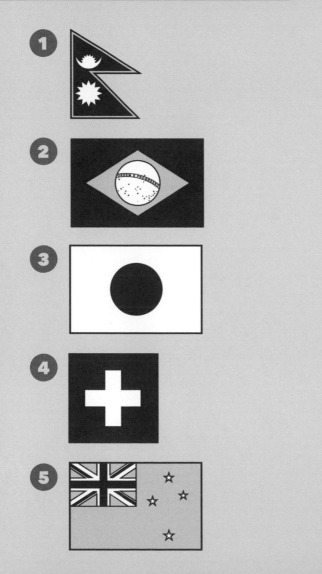

1 BRAZIL

2 NEW ZEALAND

3 NEPAL

4 SWITZERLAND

5 JAPAN

See solution on p.148

MARK DOWN

Draw a line to connect each of these landmarks with its correct country.

1 ITALY

2 EGYPT

3 USA

4 AUSTRALIA

5 UK

See solution on p.148

KNOW ALL THE
TRI-ANGLES

How many triangles can you see in the picture below?

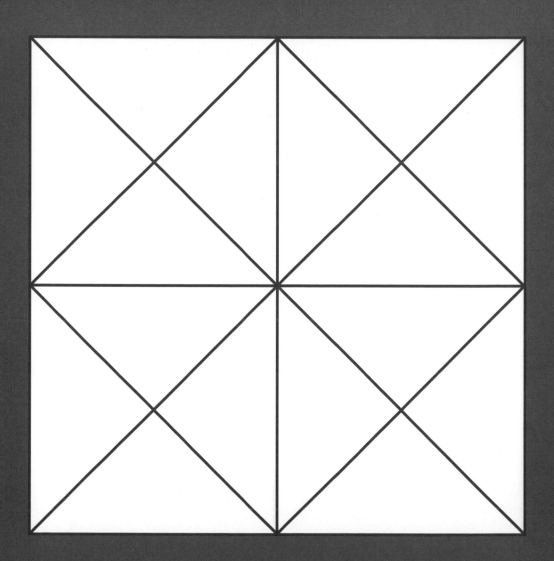

See solution on p.148

A LEOPARD CAN
CHANGE ITS SP*OTS

Can you figure out which of the big cats below is the odd one out?

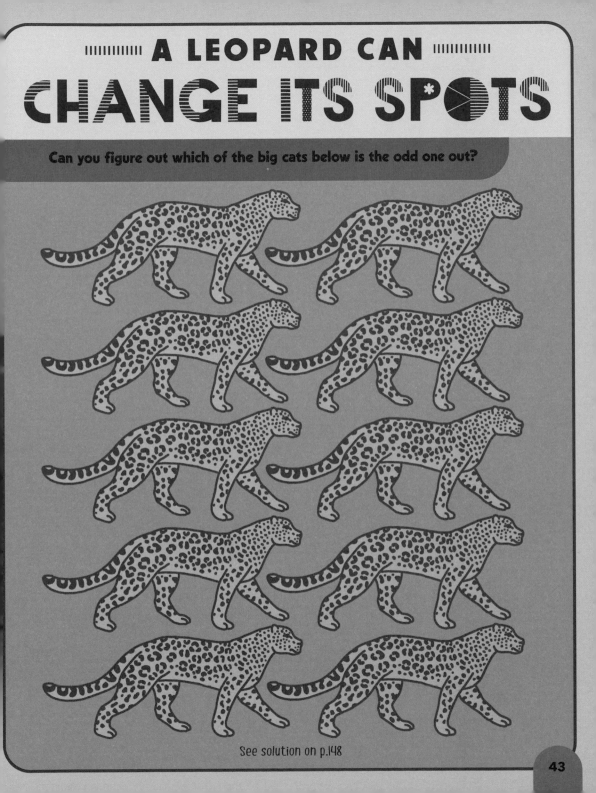

See solution on p.148

VACATION
SUDOKU

C omplete the puzzle so that each row, column, and box of six squares contains just one vacation object each.

See solution on p.148

WORKS OF ART

Fill the frames in this art gallery with pictures of things you've seen, people you've met, or activities you've done on your trip.

DOG   DUCK   FROG   HORSE   RABBIT

Can you identify the animals by their footprints? Write what you think is the correct number below each animal's name.

PIG	CHICKEN	MONKEY	CROCODILE	ELEPHANT

All these animals feed mostly on one thing. Draw a line to connect each one with its food of choice.

1 FISH

2 EUCALYPTUS LEAVES

3 ANTS

4 BAMBOO

5 HAY

CONTINENTAL
CONUNDRUMS

Can you spot the odd country out in each of these continents? Circle your answers.

EUROPE

FRANCE,   SPAIN,   CHINA,   GERMANY

~~~~~~~~~~~~~~~~~~~~~~~~~~~~~~~~~~~~~~~

ASIA

INDIA,   AUSTRALIA,   THAILAND,   MONGOLIA

~~~~~~~~~~~~~~~~~~~~~~~~~~~~~~~~~~~~~~~

SOUTH AMERICA

CANADA,   BRAZIL,   ECUADOR,   ARGENTINA

~~~~~~~~~~~~~~~~~~~~~~~~~~~~~~~~~~~~~~~

AFRICA

EGYPT,   KENYA,   NORWAY,   NIGERIA

See solution on p.149

ALL AT SEA

Can you tell which of these watery facts are true? Check the circle you think is right.

		TRUE	FALSE
1	Around 70 percent of Earth's surface is covered by water.	◯	◯
2	Over 50 percent of Earth's water is drinkable fresh water.	◯	◯
3	The world's largest ocean is the Atlantic.	◯	◯
4	The most northerly ocean is the Arctic Ocean.	◯	◯
5	The world's longest mountain range is underwater.	◯	◯

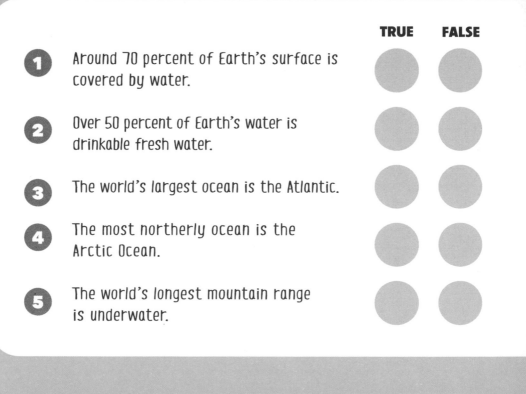

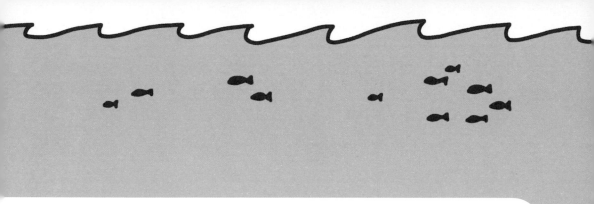

		TRUE	FALSE
6	We have explored less than 10 percent of the world's oceans.	◯	◯
7	Africa and Arabia are separated by the Black Sea.	◯	◯
8	The world's largest fish is the whale shark.	◯	◯
9	The world's largest mammal is the shark whale.	◯	◯
10	The deepest place on the face of the planet is the Mariana Trench in the Pacific Ocean.	◯	◯

EYES ON THE PRIZE

How many sunglasses can you find in the jumble below?

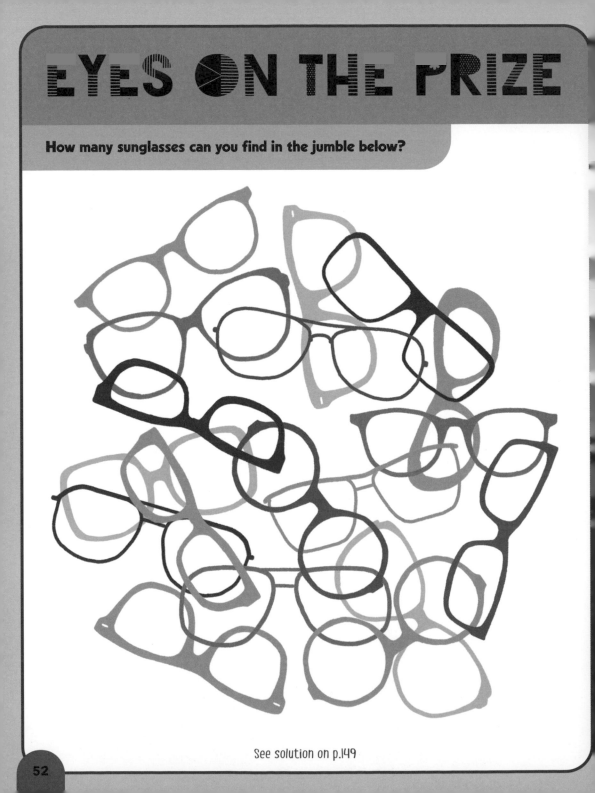

See solution on p.149

SPELL-BOUND

Find the correct letters, then spell out a word with your answers.

A H v R E K W N

1 Find a letter that's in ocean but not in volcano.

2 Find a letter that's in taxi but not in mountain.

3 Find a letter that's in ship but not in fashion.

4 Find a letter that's in motel but not in totem.

5 Find a letter that's in moon but not in camping.

6 Find a letter that's in train but not in captain.

7 Find a letter that's in museum but not in musician.

G Y M D B C
Q X C S
J Z

ANSWER:

See solution on p.149

MIND YOUR LANGUAGE

There are an estimated 7,100 spoken languages in the world. Can you find 10 of them below? Words can be found horizontally, vertically, diagonally, forward, or backward!

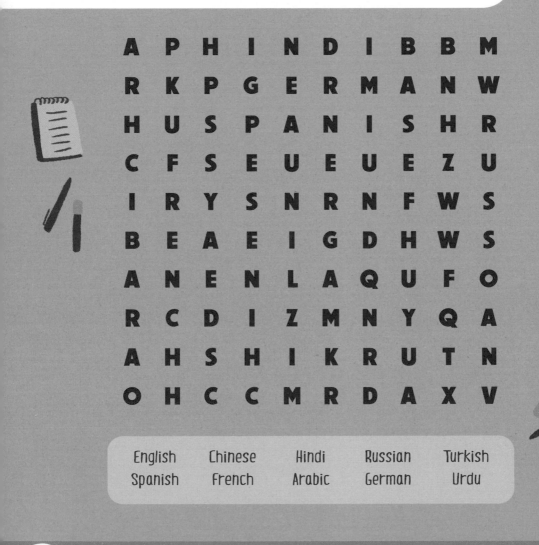

```
A P H I N D I B B M
R K P G E R M A N W
H U S P A N I S H R
C F S E U E U E Z U
I R Y S N R N F W S
B E A E I G D H W S
A N E N L A Q U F O
R C D I Z M N Y Q A
A H S H I K R U T N
O H C C M R D A X V
```

English	Chinese	Hindi	Russian	Turkish
Spanish	French	Arabic	German	Urdu

MAKE A MEAL OF IT

It might be a picnic in the park or a three-course feast.
What was your best meal out and about? Write or draw it below!

Menu

END OF THE SKY-LINE

Can you identify these cities by their skylines? Circle your answers below!

1

A) Los Angeles, USA   **B)** Boston, USA   **C)** New York, USA

2

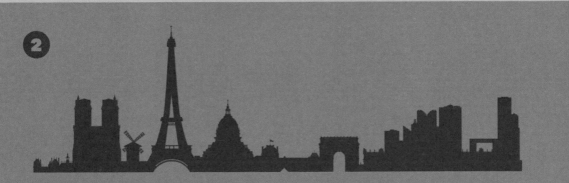

A) Amsterdam, Netherlands   **B)** Paris, France   **C)** Prague, Czech Republic

3

A) London, England   **B)** Singapore   **C)** Lagos, Nigeria

4

A) Mexico City, Mexico   **B)** Rio de Janeiro, Brazil   **C)** Caracas, Venezuela

5

A) Chicago, USA   **B)** Buenos Aires, Argentina   **C)** Dubai, United Arab Emirates

6

A) Auckland, New Zealand   **B)** Sydney, Australia   **C)** Beijing, China

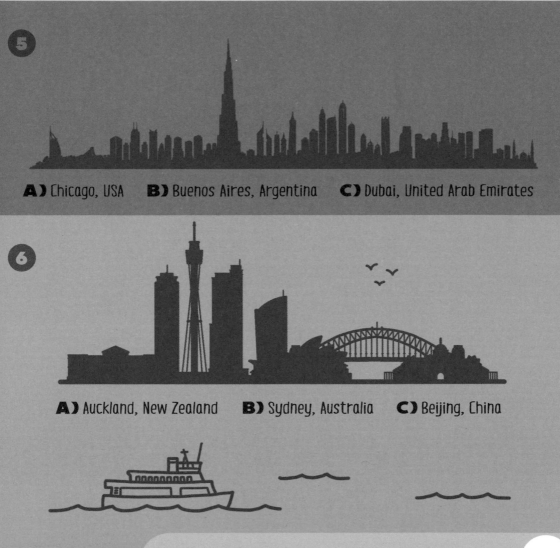

|||||||||||||||||||||||||||||||||| See solution on p.149 ||||||||||||||||||||||||

CREATURE TEACHER

In each of these three rows, one of the animals is not like the others. Can you circle the odd one out in each case?

See solution on p.150

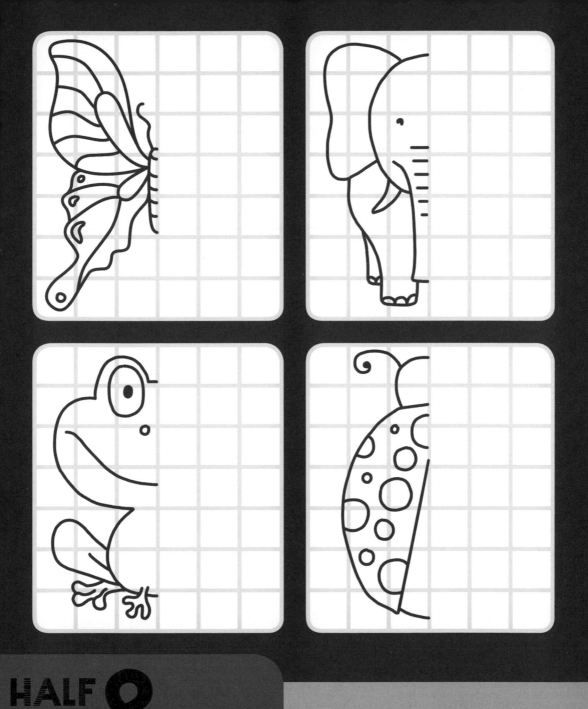

HALF & HALF

Complete the pictures of these exotic animals. The right-hand side of each image should be exactly the same as the left.

PiCK OUT THE PENGUIN

Can you spot the one penguin that isn't part of a pair?

 See solution on p.150

|||||DESTINATION||||| UNKNOWN

Jayden, Emily, Raj, and Carla are all taking a different vacation.

One is going skiing in the Swiss Alps.

One is taking a beach vacation in Florida.

One is shopping for souvenirs in New York City.

One is seeing historical sights in Rome, Italy.

Can you figure out who is going where from these clues?

- Emily is going to a city.
- Jayden is going to Europe.
- Carla and Emily are going to the USA.
- Raj is not going somewhere cold.

See solution on p.150

CRACKING THE CODE

Can you find the four broken pieces that can be put back together to make this Greek vase?

See solution on p.150

PYRAMID SCHEMING

Three blocks in this pyramid have been removed.
Can you figure out how many are left?

OFF THE MAP*

Ahoy sailor! Can you figure out which of the treasure maps on the right matches the one below?

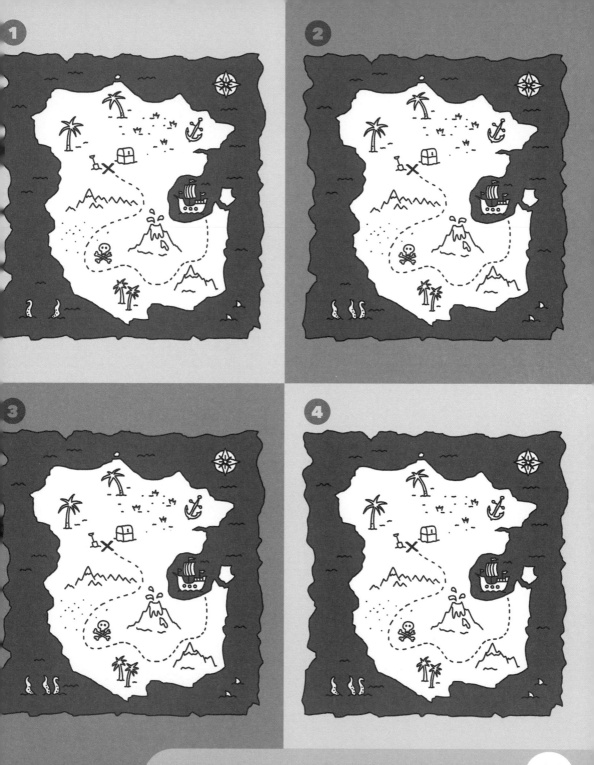

STEER CLEAR

Can you spot the one car in this parking lot that isn't like any of the others?

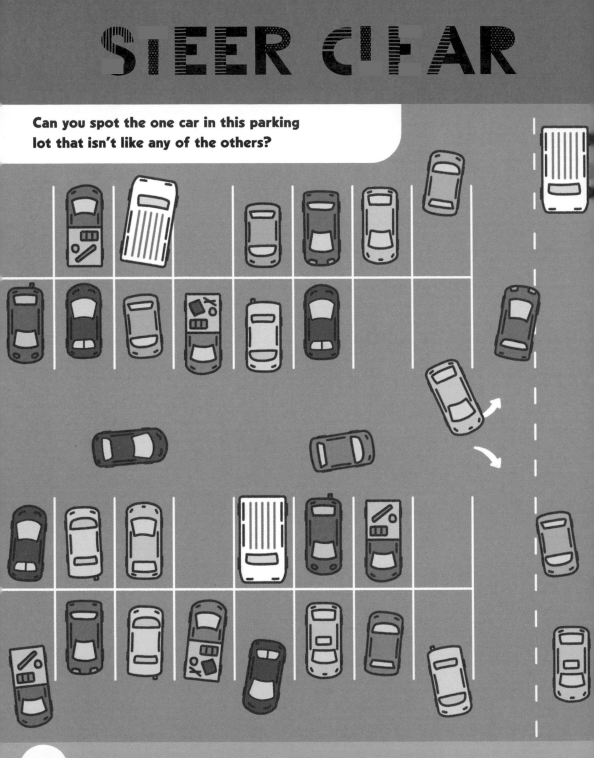

See solution on p.150

TREASURE HUNT

Mark a path to the treasure at the center of the maze.
Can you find all the different routes? Choose carefully
or you might end up back where you started!

Start

AWESOME ANIMAL

 Draw a portrait of the most impressive animal you can think of! Write its name in the space at the bottom.

SCRAMBLED CITIES

U nscramble the European capital cities in the left column, then draw a line to connect each city to the correct country!

1 asrip

_____

ITALY

2 teasdramm

_____

FRANCE

3 rinble

_____

SPAIN

4 orem

_____

NETHERLANDS

5 dramid

_____

GERMANY

See solution on p.151

BIG SCARY MONSTERS

These mythical creatures from across the world are roughly the same size. But can you use these clues to figure out which is biggest and which is smallest? Write their order of size in the spaces below.

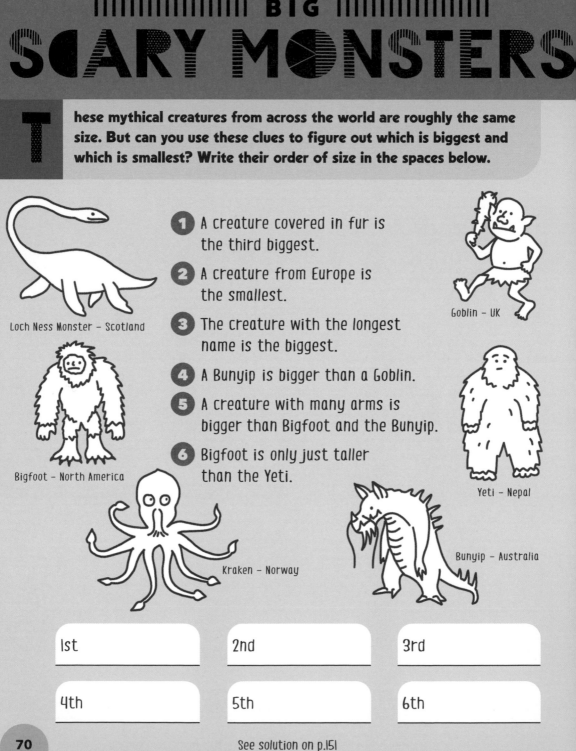

Loch Ness Monster – Scotland

Bigfoot – North America

Goblin – UK

Yeti – Nepal

Kraken – Norway

Bunyip – Australia

1. A creature covered in fur is the third biggest.

2. A creature from Europe is the smallest.

3. The creature with the longest name is the biggest.

4. A Bunyip is bigger than a Goblin.

5. A creature with many arms is bigger than Bigfoot and the Bunyip.

6. Bigfoot is only just taller than the Yeti.

1st	2nd	3rd
4th	5th	6th

See solution on p.151

TILE TEASER

Can you figure out which of the tiles below is the odd one out?

CLIMB EVERY MOUNTAIN

See if you can find all of these famous mountains and ranges in this word search. Words can be found horizontally, vertically, forward, or backward!

```
G R A N D T E T O N
F A G L O J L H J I
Z M O N T B L A N C
S W O C R A T N K J
G L E V E R E S T W
M A T T E R H O R N
W N G V O F M R U Z
H S P L A S S I W S
O E V M C W I Q L P
W X Y G R O I J U F
```

Everest   Fuji   Matterhorn
Swiss Alps   Mont Blanc   Grand Teton

See solution on p.151

UP AND AWAY

Fill the rest of the sky with flying machines. You could draw planes or helicopters or airships—or more hot-air balloons like this one, all with different shapes and patterns.

Can you spot 10 differences between these two airport scenes?

SEA, THE
MONSTER

You never know what you might see in the sea. Finish this scary monster pic by drawing its head coming out of the water on one side and its tail on the other.

YETI AGAIN

Can you figure out which silhouette is an exact match of this abominable snowman?

See solution on p.151

MOUNTAIN MATH

Can you fill in the numbers that are missing from the circles? The number in each square is the result of multiplying the numbers in the circles on either side.

See solution on p.152

Chow down! Can you draw a line from each dish to the country that it originates from?

1 TACO

2 PIZZA

3 CROISSANT

4 HAMBURGER

5 DIM SUM DUMPLINGS

6 SUSHI

FRANCE

ITALY

JAPAN

CHINA

MEXICO

USA

THE WRITING'S
ON THE WALL

Which jigsaw piece does not feature in this cave painting puzzle?

1 2 3 4 5

HIDE AND SHRIEK

an you find a surprised monkey in among all its smiling friends?

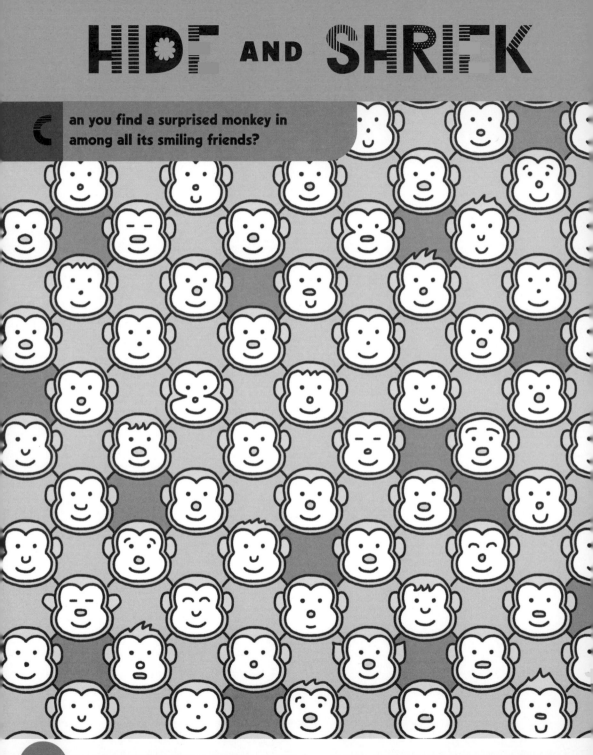

See solution on p.152

A SLOPE TO REMEMBER...

Take a long look at this skiing scene, then turn the page to see if you can remember all the details.

...WHAT'S GOING DOWN?

See what you can recall about the previous scene. Circle your answers.

1 What sort of animal was in the fir tree at the front of the scene?

A) Squirrel
B) Bird
C) Mouse

2 What color was the scarf of the person on the sled?

A) Blue
B) Red
C) Green

3 Did the houses at the back of the scene have snow on their roofs?

Yes / No

4 How many people were skiing?

A) One
B) Two
C) Three

5 The snowboarder was carrying ski poles.

True or false?

6 How many mountains were there at the back of the scene?

A) Three
B) Four
C) Five

See solution on p.152

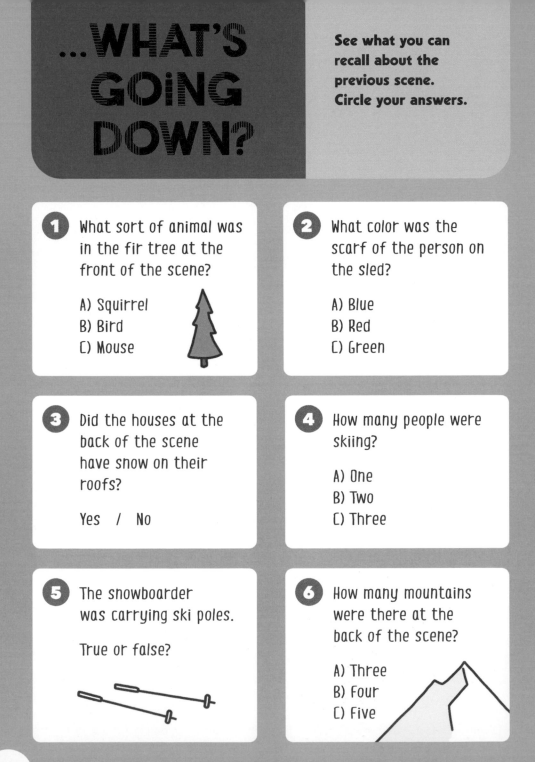

DINO DELICIOUS

Which of these dinosaurs has the biggest appetite? Solve the problems on their sides to figure out which one can eat the most.

A. $28 + 34$

B. 8×8

C. 22×3

D. $99 - 34$

E. $126 \div 2$

See solution on p.152

ANIMAL PLANET

Draw lines linking each animal to the country where it's found in the wild. There can be only one animal per country.

1 KANGAROO Brazil

2 PANDA China

3 JAGUAR Canada

4 POLAR BEAR Kenya

5 OSTRICH Australia

See solution on p.152

IT'S ALL GREEK

How many triangles, squares, and rectangles can you spot in this ancient Greek temple?

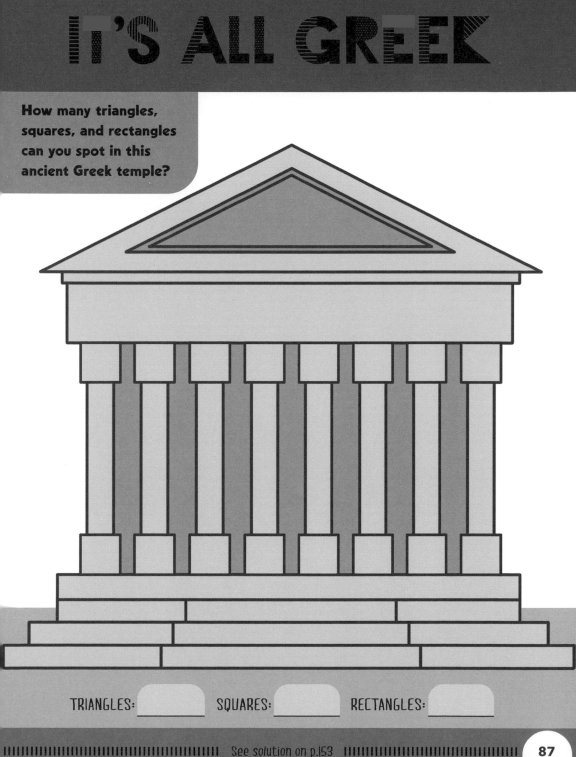

TRIANGLES: SQUARES: RECTANGLES:

See solution on p.153

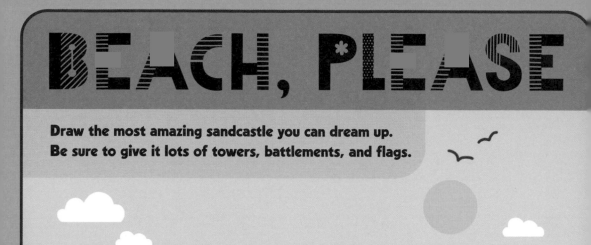

BEACH, PLEASE

Draw the most amazing sandcastle you can dream up.
Be sure to give it lots of towers, battlements, and flags.

STREETWISE

How well do you know your cities? See if you can match each city to its description. Write your answers in the spaces.

1 I am famous for my Day of the Dead celebrations.

_____

2 Table Mountain overlooks me.

_____

3 Sometimes I'm called the Big Apple.

_____

4 You'll find the Forbidden City here.

_____

5 The Seine River runs through me.

_____

BEIJING   PARIS   NEW YORK   MEXICO CITY   CAPE TOWN

See solution on p.153

GIVE IT YOUR BEST SHOT

Know your sports? Figure out which statements are fact or fiction below.

		TRUE	FALSE
1	All racehorses have the same official birthday, no matter when they're born.	○	○
2	The national sport of Japan is sumo wrestling.	○	○
3	The Tour de France is a running event.	○	○
4	Brazil has won the men's FIFA soccer World Cup five times, more than any other country.	○	○
5	There are eight events in a decathlon.	○	○

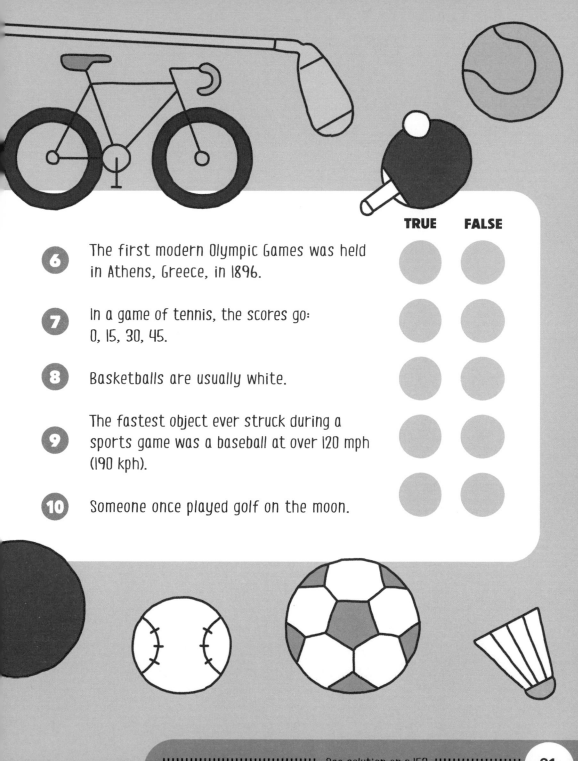

		TRUE	FALSE
6	The first modern Olympic Games was held in Athens, Greece, in 1896.	○	○
7	In a game of tennis, the scores go: 0, 15, 30, 45.	○	○
8	Basketballs are usually white.	○	○
9	The fastest object ever struck during a sports game was a baseball at over 120 mph (190 kph).	○	○
10	Someone once played golf on the moon.	○	○

See solution on p.153

A-MAZE-ING
CITY

Draw a path through this city maze, avoiding the buildings.

START ▶

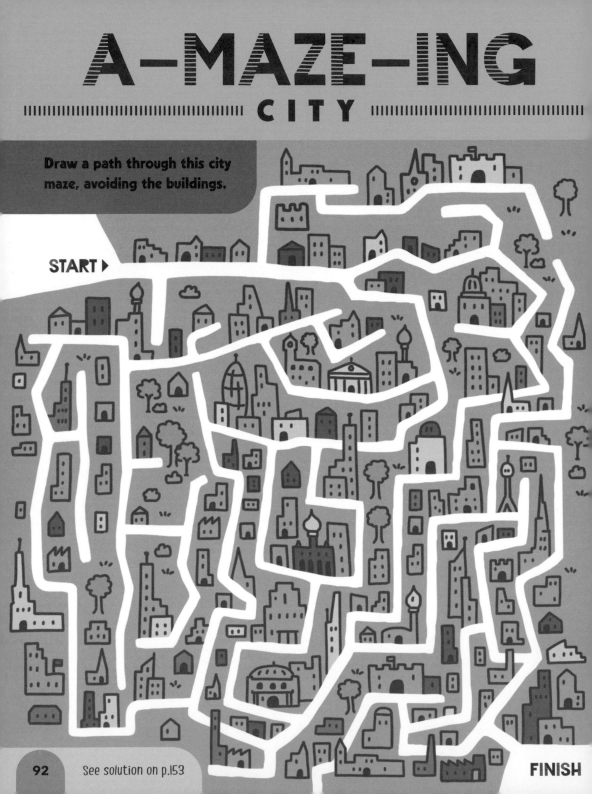

See solution on p.153

FINISH

BENEATH THE SURFACE

Draw what you think this diver can see down below the waves. It could be starfish, sharks, crabs, coral, or maybe even monsters.

MAKE A BEELINE FOR IT

Can you figure out which bee has flown from which hive?

See solution on p.153

Are you able to match the correct lower half of this matryoshka (or nesting) doll with its top half?

1

2

3

4

5

6

7

See solution on p.153

MUDDLED MONUMENTS

Unscramble these famous landmarks, and then draw lines to connect them to the country where they can be found.

1 cluesmoos

_____ ○   ○ UNITED KINGDOM

2 retag lalw

_____ ○   ○ ITALY

3 phornetna

_____ ○   ○ CHINA

4 wtero fo dolnon

_____ ○   ○ UNITED STATES

5 atsuet fo bretily

_____ ○   ○ GREECE

 See solution on p.153

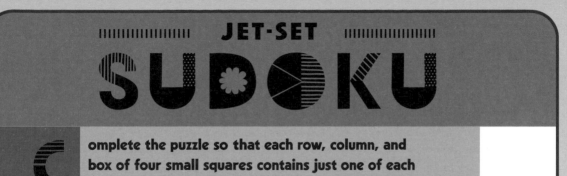

JET-SET SUDOKU

Complete the puzzle so that each row, column, and box of four small squares contains just one of each of the following things you might see at the airport.

See solution on p.153

WORK YOUR MAGIC

Can you find these 10 items hidden around the magic castle? Circle the objects when you find them.

RABBIT

SHIP

CROWN

SEA MONSTER

3-PETAL FLOWER

SHIELD

UNICORN

PRINCESS

FROG

FIR TREE

JUST FOCUS

Can you figure out which of the squares on the left isn't featured in the picture of the camera below? Circle your answer.

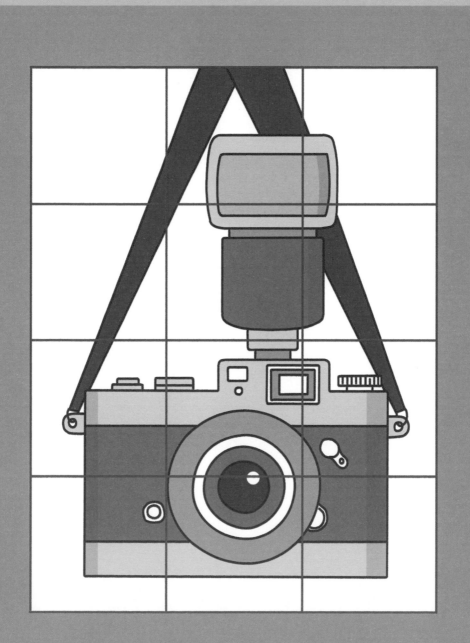

MIXED-UP METROPOLISES

Unscramble the capital cities in the left column, then draw a line to connect each city to the correct country!

1 hastingnow cd

_____ ●   ● NEW ZEALAND

2 nongewltil

_____ ●   ● CHINA

3 wen heldi

_____ ●   ● USA

4 jinbeig

_____ ●   ● INDIA

5 bosenu raies

_____ ●   ● ARGENTINA

See solution on p.154

CRAWL SPACE

I magine turning over a rock and looking at lots of creepy-crawlies through a magnifying glass. Draw all the different bugs you can see—you could even invent some new ones.

WATERY WORD SEARCH

Most of the surface of the Earth is water! Find all the oceans and rivers listed in the word search below.

```
H H I N D I A N W I
A G S E I N E O S N
D A N U B E L H I D
N N P A C I F I C U
I G Q A C W T V X S
L E F X A R C T I C
E S L R A M A Z O N
C H A N G J I A N G
Y A T L A N T I C M
P L S O U T H E R N
```

Chang Jiang	Arctic	Amazon	Indus
Southern	Indian	Atlantic	Seine
Pacific	Danube	Ganges	Nile

Draw the face that could be wearing this hat and sunglasses. You can base it on someone you know or make up their features using your imagination.

FiNS AIN'T WHAT THEY USED TO BE

Can you figure out which silhouette is an exact match of this scuba diver?

BUDGET BREAKAWAY

Can you figure out what each of these vacation items cost? Fill in your answers below.

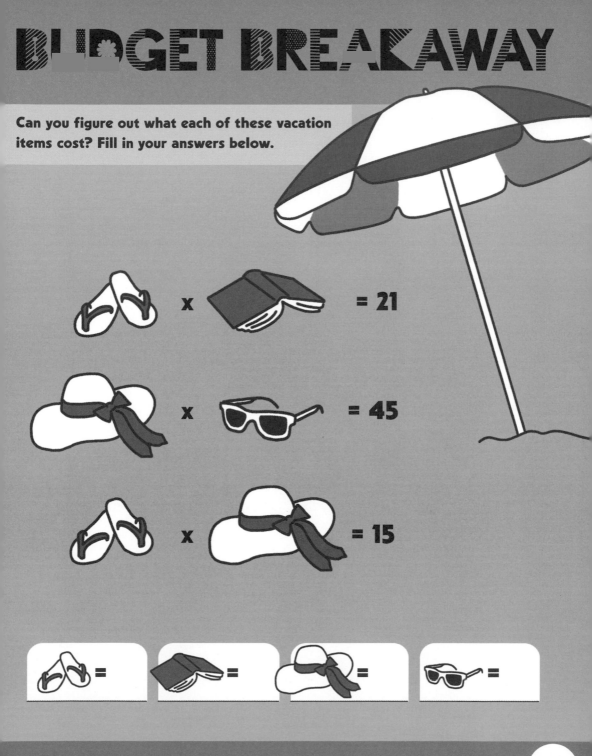

x = 21

x = 45

x = 15

=

=

=

=

See solution on p.155

SEA YOU LATER

How many fish can you see in this underwater scene? Draw a circle around every one you can find, then write your answer in the box.

Answer:

Which of these camels has recently stopped for a drink at a desert oasis?

EARN YOUR STRIPES*

E very zebra forms part of a pair, except one. Can you find the zebra with a unique set of stripes?

See solution on p.155

SIMPLI-CITY ITSELF

Can you identify these cities by their skylines? Circle your answers below!

1

A) Nairobi, Kenya   **B)** Naples, Italy   **C)** Tokyo, Japan

2

A) Stockholm, Sweden   **B)** Moscow, Russia   **C)** Helsinki, Finland

3

A) Lisbon, Portugal   **B)** Rome, Italy   **C)** Barcelona, Spain

4

A) Cairo, Egypt   **B)** Marrakesh, Morocco   **C)** Athens, Greece

5

A) Kuala Lumpur, Malaysia   **B)** Shanghai, China   **C)** New Delhi, India

6

A) Madrid, Spain   **B)** Toronto, Canada   **C)** Lima, Peru

See solution on p.155

BOUNCING BACK

Draw lines to connect each of the balls below with its sport.

1
2
3
4
5
6

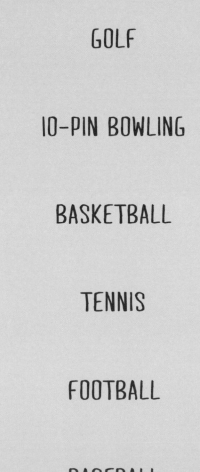

GOLF

10-PIN BOWLING

BASKETBALL

TENNIS

FOOTBALL

BASEBALL

||||| GET THE ||||| SCOOP*

Mo, Danny, and Lara are buying ice-cream cones. One has ordered three scoops, another has ordered two scoops, and the other has ordered one scoop. Each ice-cream cone has a different topping. One has multicolored sprinkles, another has strawberry sauce, and the other has chocolate chips.

Can you figure out who has ordered what from these clues? Write your answers in the boxes below.

- Mo has more scoops than Danny.
- Danny did not order chocolate chips.
- The ice cream with multicolored sprinkles has the most scoops.
- The ice cream with chocolate chips has the fewest scoops.

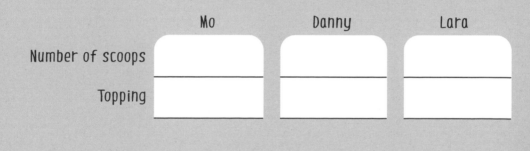

	Mo	Danny	Lara
Number of scoops			
Topping			

See solution on p.156

Changing Rooms

Can you spot 10 differences between these two poolside scenes?

See solution on p.156

MATCH THE FLAGS

Draw a line to connect each of the flags below with its correct country.

CANADA

TURKEY

KENYA

WALES

SOUTH AFRICA

See solution on p.156

FLY YOUR FLAG

Design a flag for your vacation that shows off all the cool things you've done.

LOST IN THE RAINFOREST

Lurking in the darkest corners of this word search are things associated with the Amazon rainforest! Can you find all the words listed below?

```
Q A C T M A C A W Q
M P N A R L C Z E J
A A I A P G F N L D
N T H R C Y I A L U
A S O O A O B T N E
T L J U G N N A Q T
E O F B C A H D R K
E T B E Z A N A A A
O H Y T W G N Y T N
T A R A N T U L A D
```

tarantula   capybara   piranha   sloth   manatee
anaconda   mahogany   toucan   ant   macaw

See solution on p.156

||||||| ALL ||||||| SQUARE

Outline all the squares you can see in this picture. There may be more than you think!

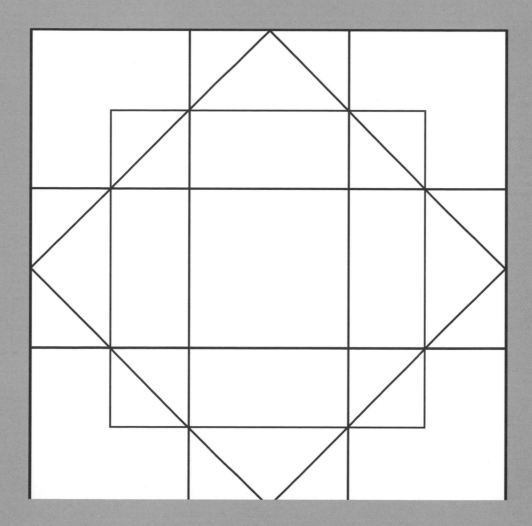

ICE SPLICE

C an you untangle the lines to figure out which item has been dropped by which ice skater?

FLYING COLORS

These kites form a sequence.

Which of the below images would be next in the sequence?

See solution on p.157

COUNTRY CLUES

How well do you know the countries of the world? Separate the true from the false in the statements below. Check off your answers.

		TRUE	FALSE
1	The world's biggest country by area is Canada.	◯	◯
2	The world's smallest country by area is the Vatican City.	◯	◯
3	Every piece of land on Earth forms part of—or is owned by—a country.	◯	◯
4	The currency of Japan is the euro.	◯	◯
5	There are no mosquitoes in Iceland.	◯	◯

		TRUE	FALSE
6	There are over 50 countries in Africa.	○	○
7	Most of the Amazon rainforest is found in Brazil.	○	○
8	The world's longest river, the Nile, reaches the sea in Egypt.	○	○
9	The capital of Australia is Sydney.	○	○
10	There are over 50 countries in South America.	○	○

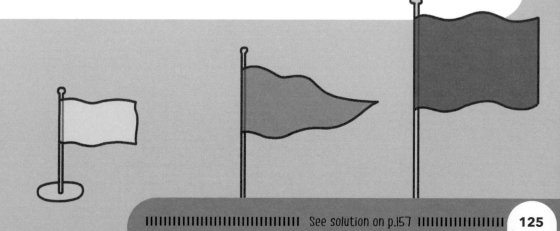

See solution on p.157

LUGGAGE LEARNING

Can you figure out which luggage belongs to which traveler by solving these math problems?

220 ÷ 22

48 − 42

7

9

6

22 + 34 ÷ 8

128 ÷ 2 ÷ 8

63 ÷ 7

8

10

126   See solution on p.157

RUNWAY RULER

an you separate these planes so each has its own separate zone by drawing just three straight lines across the page? There should be just one plane per zone.

See solution on p.157

CONCRETE JUNGLE
|||||||||||||| #ONE ||||||||||||||

How well do you know your cities? See if you can match each city to its description. Write your answers in the spaces.

1 A great fire in 1666 almost wiped me out.

_____

2 I am the world's highest capital city.

_____

3 I have the biggest population in the world, and I'm close to an active volcano called Mount Fuji.

_____

4 I am known for my opera house.

_____

5 I am an ancient city in the Himalayas.

_____

SYDNEY   LA PAZ   KATHMANDU   LONDON   TOKYO

See solution on p.157

STICK AT IT

Using stick figures is a great way to quickly capture a busy scene. Draw the people you can see around you—or make up a scene—using only stick figures for both people and animals.

IN A SPIN

Can you figure out which silhouette is an exact match of this helicopter? Circle your answer.

See solution on p.157

NOW YOU SEE IT...

Carefully study this picture of a play area. When you think you've got it memorized, turn the page to see if you can spot what's missing.

...NOW YOU DON'T

Can you spot eight objects from the previous page that aren't there any more? If you get stuck, you can check back to see if you can spot what the differences are.

See solution on p.158

CATCH THE
CHAMELEON'S EYE

All these chameleons are looking the same way—except for one.
Can you find the lizard that's not quite like the others?

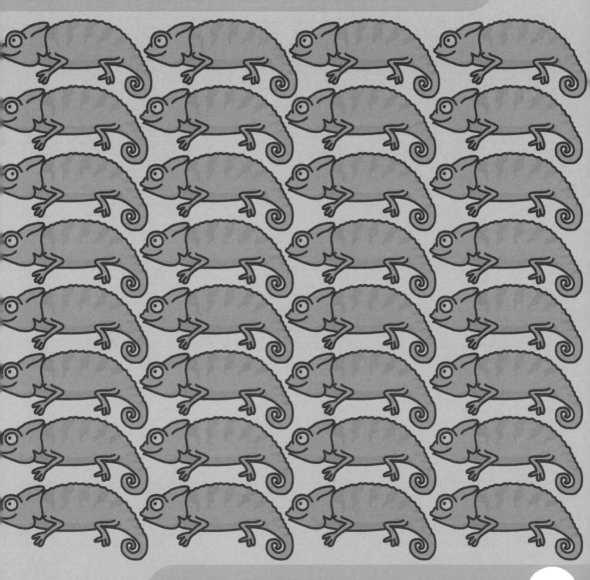

JUNGLE FEVER

Can you spot these animals hiding among the trees of the Amazon rainforest? Circle them when you find them.

A MACAW

A SLOTH

A SQUIRREL MONKEY

4 FROGS

3 BUTTERFLIES

A JAGUAR

2 SNAKES

CONCRETE JUNGLE
|||||||||||||| #TWO ||||||||||||||

Here are some more cities to identify. See if you can match the descriptions to the cities. Write your answers in the spaces.

1 I'm known for my ancient Colosseum.

_____

2 I contain a giant complex called the Forbidden City.

_____

3 I'm home to the Hollywood movie industry.

_____

4 My name means "good airs" in Spanish.

_____

5 I'm the capital of Kenya.

_____

BUENOS AIRES   LOS ANGELES   BEIJING   NAIROBI   ROME

See solution on p.159

CLOUD-O-METER

What's the weather like today?
Draw the cloud pattern you see in the sky!

SHOW YOUR CARDS

Greetings from

Then design a stamp to mail it.

Design your own postcard on the left-hand page, featuring a special place or activity from your trip. Then write the messages you'd like to send below.

WINDOW SPOTTING

How many windows can you spot in this city scene? Don't forget to count the car windows and windows that are partly hidden. Write the number in the box.

Answer:

See solution on p.159

SPAGHETTI
JUNCTION

Who is eating which bowl of pasta?

A WHEEL DIFFERENCE

In each of these rows, one of the vehicles is not like the others.
Can you circle the odd one out in each case?

1

2

3

4

See solution on p.159

FOLLOW YOUR STAR

Create your own constellation.
Make a shape by connecting stars on the grid below.

PYRAMID PILEUP

 an you figure out what the sequence is on these pyramids and fill in the blanks?

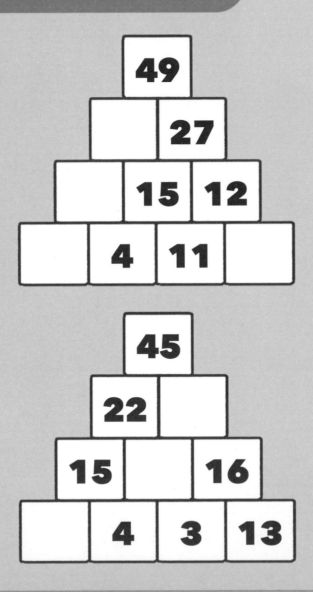

ANSWERS

ANSWERS

p.6 A Whole New Ball Game

There are 10 balls.

pp.8-9 Top (Land) Marks

1. Statue of Liberty, USA
2. Colosseum, Italy
3. Taj Mahal, India
4. Tower Bridge, UK
5. Pyramids of Giza, Egypt
6 Christ the Redeemer, Brazil
7. Eiffel Tower, France
8. Sydney Opera House, Australia
9. Chichén Itza, Mexico
10. Great Wall of China
11. Sagrada Familia, Spain
12. Burj Khalifa, UAE
13. Angkor Wat, Cambodia
14. Mount Rushmore, USA
15. Table Mountain, South Africa
16. Acropolis, Greece

pp.10-11 Blank Check

1. red
2. yellow
3. gondola
4. ship
5. Wright
6. sleds
7. steam
8. airship

p.12 It's No Picnic

p.13 Continent Content

1. South America
2. Africa
3. Asia
4. Europe

p.14 Squared Up

There are 11 squares.

pp.16-17 Just Deserts

1. False. They cover about a third of Earth's land surface.
2. False. Around 80 percent of deserts aren't sandy.
3. True
4. False. In cold deserts, it often snows.
5. True. There are parts of the Atacama Desert in South America where no rainfall has been recorded.
6. True
7. False. It doesn't often rain in deserts, but when it does, it can rain a lot. The ground is often hard, stopping the water from seeping through, which causes floods.
8. False. Deserts are usually sparsely populated but many have populations of people.
9. True
10. False. Cacti only grow naturally in the Americas

p.18 Out of the Air

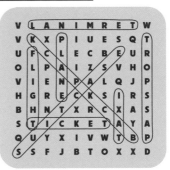

pp.20-21 Numbers Up

1. 11, 13, 15 (ascending odd numbers)
2. 51, 61, 71 (+10)
3. 26, 31, 36 (+5)
4. 16, 22, 29 (+5, +6, +7)
5. 14, 8, 1 (-5, -6, -7)
6. 13, 21, 34 (each number is the sum of the two numbers preceding it)
7. 96, 192, 384 (x2)
8. 22, 15, 8 (-7)
9. 243, 729, 2187 (x3)
10. 16, 8, 4 (÷ 2)

p.24 Away from the Pack

The towel didn't fit in.

pp.26-27 Search in the Woods

p.28 Lost Luggage

p.29 Course from the Source

1. –> C
2. –> B
3. –> D
4. –> A

p.30 Stuck in Traffic

Tile 3 doesn't appear in the scene.

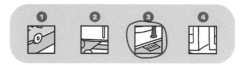

p.31 Ship Shape

Ship 5 is an exact match.

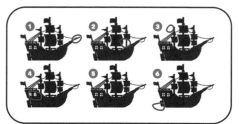

p.32 Jewel School

Two yellow jewels:
Red jewel = 6
Green Jewel = 3
Blue Jewel = 2
Yellow jewel = 1

p.34 Check Out

1. B) 3 o'clock
2. False
3. Six keys
4. B) A bell
5. Red and blue

p.35 Winging It

ANSWERS

p.38 That's Capital

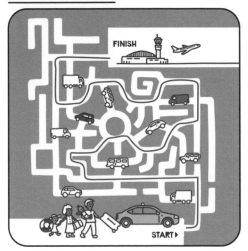

p.39 Plane and Simple

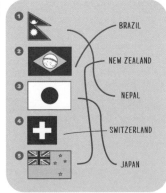

p.40 Flag Up

1. → NEPAL
2. → BRAZIL
3. → JAPAN
4. → SWITZERLAND
5. → NEW ZEALAND

p.41 Mark Down

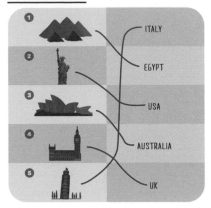

1. → EGYPT
2. → USA
3. → AUSTRALIA
4. → UK
5. → ITALY

p.42 Know All the Tri-Angles

There are 44 triangles.

p.43 A Leopard Can Change Its Spots

p.44 Vacation Sudoku

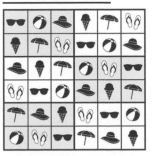

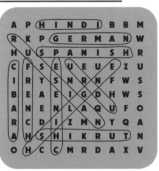

pp.46-47 On the Right Tracks

Dog: 3
Duck: 6
Frog: 1
Horse: 9
Rabbit: 7

Pig: 10
Chicken: 2
Monkey: 8
Crocodile: 4
Elephant: 5

p.48 Critter Cravings

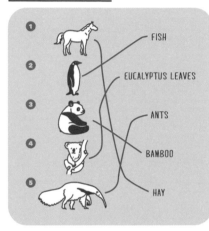

p.49 Continental Conundrums

Europe: China (which is in Asia)
Asia: Australia (which is a continent in its own right)
South America: Canada (which is in North America)
Africa: Norway (which is in Europe)

pp.50-51 All at Sea

1. True
2. False. Just 3 percent of Earth's water is fresh water.
3. False. It's the Pacific.
4. True
5. True. The Mid-Ocean Ridge stretches for about 40,000 miles (65,000 km) right around the world beneath the water's surface.
6. True
7. False. They're separated by the Red Sea.
8. True
9. False. It's the blue whale.
10. True. It descends to a depth of around 36,037 ft. (10,984 m).

p.52 Eyes on the Prize

There are 18 pairs of glasses.

p.53 Spell Bound

1. e
2. x
3. p
4. l
5. o
6. r
7. e
Answer: explore

p.54 Mind Your Language

pp.56-57 End of the Sky-Line

1. C) New York, USA
2. B) Paris, France
3. A) London, England
4. B) Rio de Janeiro, Brazil
5. C) Dubai, United Arab Emirates
6. B) Sydney, Australia

ANSWERS

p.58 Creature Teacher

1. Ostrich – it can't fly.

2 Kangaroo – it hops on two legs while the others walk on four legs.

3 Spider – it has eight legs, while the insects have six.

p.60 Pick Out the Penguin

p.61 Destination Unknown

Jayden is going to the Swiss Alps.

Emily is going to New York.

Raj is going to Rome.

Carla is going to Florida.

p.62 Cracking the Code

Pieces 1, 3, 5, and 7 can be put back together to make the vase.

p.63 Pyramid Scheming

382. The bottom row is a square of 10 x 10 cubes (100 cubes).
Each row above that has one less cube per side until
there's just one on top. So 10 x 10 (100) + 9 x 9 (81) + 8 x 8
(64) + 7 x 7 (49) + 6 x 6 (36) + 5 x 5 (25) + 4 x 4 (16) +
3 x 3 (9) + 2 x 2 (4) + 1 = 385. Minus the three missing
cubes = 382.

p.64 Off the Map

Number 3 is the exact match.

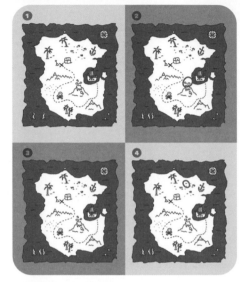

p.66 Steer Clear

p.67 Treasure Hunt

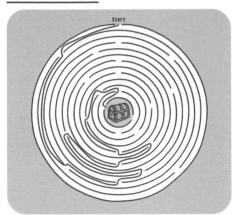

p.69 Scrambled Cities

1. Paris –> France
2. Amsterdam –> Netherlands
3. Berlin –> Germany
4. Rome –> Italy
5. Madrid –> Spain

p.70 Big Scary Monsters

1st biggest: Loch Ness Monster, Scotland
2nd biggest: Bigfoot, North America
3rd biggest: Yeti, Nepal
4th biggest: Kraken, Norway
5th biggest: Bunyip, Australia
6th biggest: Goblin, England

p.71 Tile Teaser

p.72 Climb Every Mountain

pp.74-75 Hiding in Plane Sight

p.78 Yeti Again

Number 3 is an exact match.

ANSWERS

p.79 Mountain Math

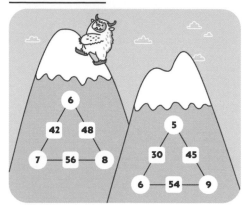

p.80 Food for Thought

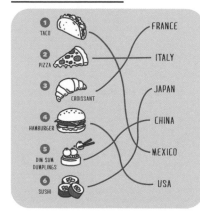

p.81 The Writing's On the Wall

Piece 4 doesn't feature in the cave painting.

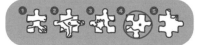

p.82 Hide and Shriek

p.84 What's Going Down?

1. B) Bird
2. A) Blue
3. Yes
4. B) Two

5. False. Only the skiers were carrying poles.
6. C) Five

p.85 Dino Delicious

A) 28 + 34 = 62
B) 8 x 8 = 64
C) 22 x 3 = 66 – this one, the Triceratops, ate the most.

D) 99 – 34 = 65
E) 126 ÷ 2 = 63

p.86 Animal Planet

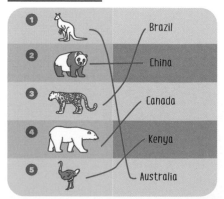

p.87 It's All Greek

Triangles: 3   Rectangles: 20

Squares: 16

p.89 Streetwise

1. Mexico City
2. Cape Town
3. New York
4. Beijing
5. Paris

pp.90-91 Give It Your Best Shot

1. True. All horses in the northern hemisphere have an official birthday of January 1, while those in the southern hemisphere have an official birthday of August 1.

2. True

3. False. It's a cycling competition.

4. True

5. False. There are 10 events.

6. True

7. False. They go 0, 15, 30, 40.

8. False. They are usually orange.

9. False. Although baseballs have been hit at over 120 mph (190 kph), golf balls have been hit at over 211 mph (340 kph). However, the fastest object ever struck during a sports game was a shuttlecock at 306 mph (493 kph) in a game of badminton.

10. True. In 1971, Alan Shepard took a golf club and two balls on the Apollo 14 mission to the moon.

p.92 A-Maze-Ing City

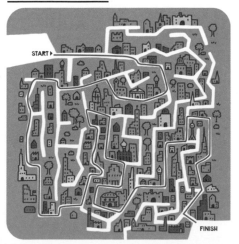

p.94 Make a Beeline for It

1. -> D
2. -> A
3. -> C
4. -> B

p.95 Dolled Up

Number 5 is the correct lower half.

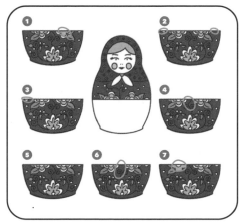

p.96 Muddled Monuments

1. Colosseum -> Italy
2. Great Wall -> China
3. Parthenon -> Greece
4. Tower of London -> UK
5. Statue of Liberty -> USA

p.97 Jet-Set Sudoku

153

ANSWERS

pp.98-99 Work Your Magic

p.104 Watery Word Search

pp.100-101 Just Focus

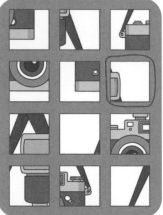

p.102 Mixed-Up Metropolises

1. Washington, DC –> USA
2. Wellington –> New Zealand
3. New Delhi –> India
4. Beijing –> China
5. Buenos Aires –> Argentina

p.106 Fins Ain't What They Used to Be

Number 2 is an exact match.

p.107 Budget Breakaway

154

pp.108-109 Sea You Later

There are 20 fish.

p.110 Dearly Deserted

Camel 3 has recently stopped for a drink.

p.111 Earn Your Stripes

Zebra D has a unique set of stripes.

pp.112-113 Simpli-City Itself

1. C) Tokyo, Japan
2. B) Moscow, Russia
3. C) Barcelona, Spain
4. A) Cairo, Egypt
5. A) Kuala Lumpur, Malaysia
6. B) Toronto, Canada

ANSWERS

p.114 Bouncing Back

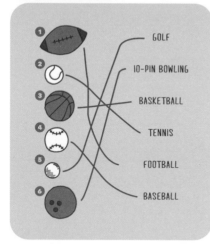

1 ——— FOOTBALL
2 ——— TENNIS
3 ——— BASKETBALL
4 ——— BASEBALL
5 ——— GOLF
6 ——— 10-PIN BOWLING

GOLF
10-PIN BOWLING
BASKETBALL
TENNIS
FOOTBALL
BASEBALL

p.115 Get the Scoop

Mo has ordered three scoops with multicolored sprinkles.
Danny has ordered two scoops with strawberry sauce.
Lara has ordered one scoop with chocolate chips.

pp.116-117 Different Strokes

p.118 Match the Flags

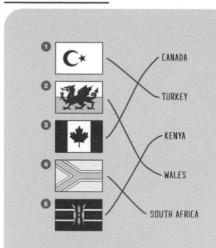

1 ——— TURKEY
2 ——— WALES
3 ——— CANADA
4 ——— SOUTH AFRICA
5 ——— KENYA

CANADA
TURKEY
KENYA
WALES
SOUTH AFRICA

p.120 Lost in the Rainforest

p.121 All Square

There are 24 squares in total.

p.122 Ice Splice

1. –> B (woolly hat)   3. –> A (scarf)
2. –> D (earmuffs)   4. –> C (gloves)

p.123 Flying Colors

Number I would be next in the sequence. The colors on the kite are moving around clockwise each turn, while the colors on the tail are moving around counterclockwise each turn.

pp.124-125 Country Clues

1. False. It's Russia. Canada is the second biggest.
2. True
3. False. Antarctica and a few small territories are not owned by any country.
4. False. It's the yen.
5. True
6. True. There are 54.
7. True
8. True
9. False. It's Canberra.
10. False. There are just 12 countries in South America.

p.126 Luggage Learning

$220 \div 22 = 10$

$48 - 42 = 6$

$22 + 34 \div 8 = 7$

$128 \div 2 \div 8 = 8$

$63 \div 7 = 9$

p.127 Runway Ruler

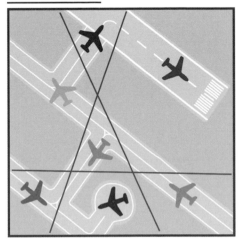

p.128 Concrete Jungle—One

1. London
2. La Paz
3. Tokyo
4. Sydney
5. Kathmandu

p.130 In a Spin

Number 3 is an exact match.

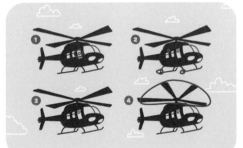

ANSWERS

p.132 Now You Don't

p.133 Catch the Chameleon's Eye

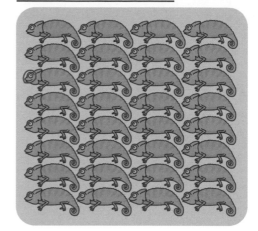

pp.134-135 Jungle Fever

p.136 Concrete Jungle—Two

1. Rome
2. Beijing
3. Los Angeles
4. Buenos Aires
5. Nairobi

p.140 Window Spotting

There are 71 windows.

p.141 Spaghetti Junction

1. → D
2. → B
3. → A
4. → C

p.142 A Wheel Difference

1. Boat – it travels on water, while the other three vehicles fly in the air.
2. Car – it has four wheels, while the other vehicles have two wheels.
3. Truck – it carries goods, while the other three vehicles carry passengers.
4. Motorboat – it's powered by a motor, while the other three vehicles are people-powered.

p.144 Pyramid Pileup

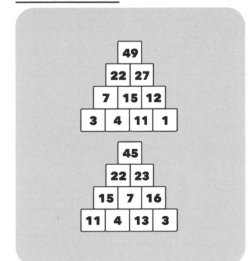

Pairs of numbers in one row add up to the number in the block directly above. So 11 + 4 = 15, 4 + 3 = 7, 3 + 13 = 16, and so on.

NOTES AND SCRIBBLES

Use this page to figure out any math or logic puzzles that are proving tricky.